NEW ORLEANS SAINTS

BY PHIL ERVIN

SportsZone
An Imprint of Abdo Publishing
abdopublishing.com

abdopublishing.com

Published by Abdo Publishing, a division of ABDO, PO Box 398166, Minneapolis, Minnesota 55439. Copyright © 2017 by Abdo Consulting Group, Inc. International copyrights reserved in all countries. No part of this book may be reproduced in any form without written permission from the publisher. SportsZone™ is a trademark and logo of Abdo Publishing.

Printed in the United States of America, North Mankato, Minnesota
042016
092016

THIS BOOK CONTAINS RECYCLED MATERIALS

Cover Photo: Ross D. Franklin/AP Images
Interior Photos: Ross D. Franklin/AP Images, 1; Mark J. Terrill/AP Images, 4-5; Mike Groll/AP Images, 6; David J. Phillip/AP Images, 7, 25; Eric Gay/AP Images, 8-9; NFL Photos/AP Images, 10-11, 15; AP Images, 12-13, 14; Vernon Biever/AP Images, 16-17; Tennen Maury/AP Images, 18-19; David Longstreath/AP Images, 20-21; Bill Haber/AP Images, 22-23; Alex Brandon/AP Images, 24; Bill Feig/AP Images, 26-27; Kevin Terrell/AP Images, 28-29

Editor: Todd Kortemeier
Series Designer: Nikki Farinella

Cataloging-in-Publication Data
Names: Ervin, Phil, author.
Title: New Orleans Saints / by Phil Ervin.
Description: Minneapolis, MN : Abdo Publishing, [2017] | Series: NFL up close | Includes index.
Identifiers: LCCN 2015960439 | ISBN 9781680782257 (lib. bdg.) | ISBN 9781680776362 (ebook)
Subjects: LCSH: New Orleans Saints (Football team)--History--Juvenile literature. | National Football League--Juvenile literature. | Football--Juvenile literature. | Professional sports--Juvenile literature. | Football teams--Louisiana--Juvenile literature.
Classification: DDC 796.332--dc23
LC record available at http://lccn.loc.gov/2015960439

TABLE OF CONTENTS

SUPER SAINTS 4

BEGINNINGS 10

DOWN YEARS 14

MARCHING IN 18

STORMS AND SUCCESSES 24

Timeline 30
Glossary 31
Index / About the Author 32

FAST FACT

Quarterback Drew Brees began his career with the San Diego Chargers. He signed with New Orleans as a free agent in 2006.

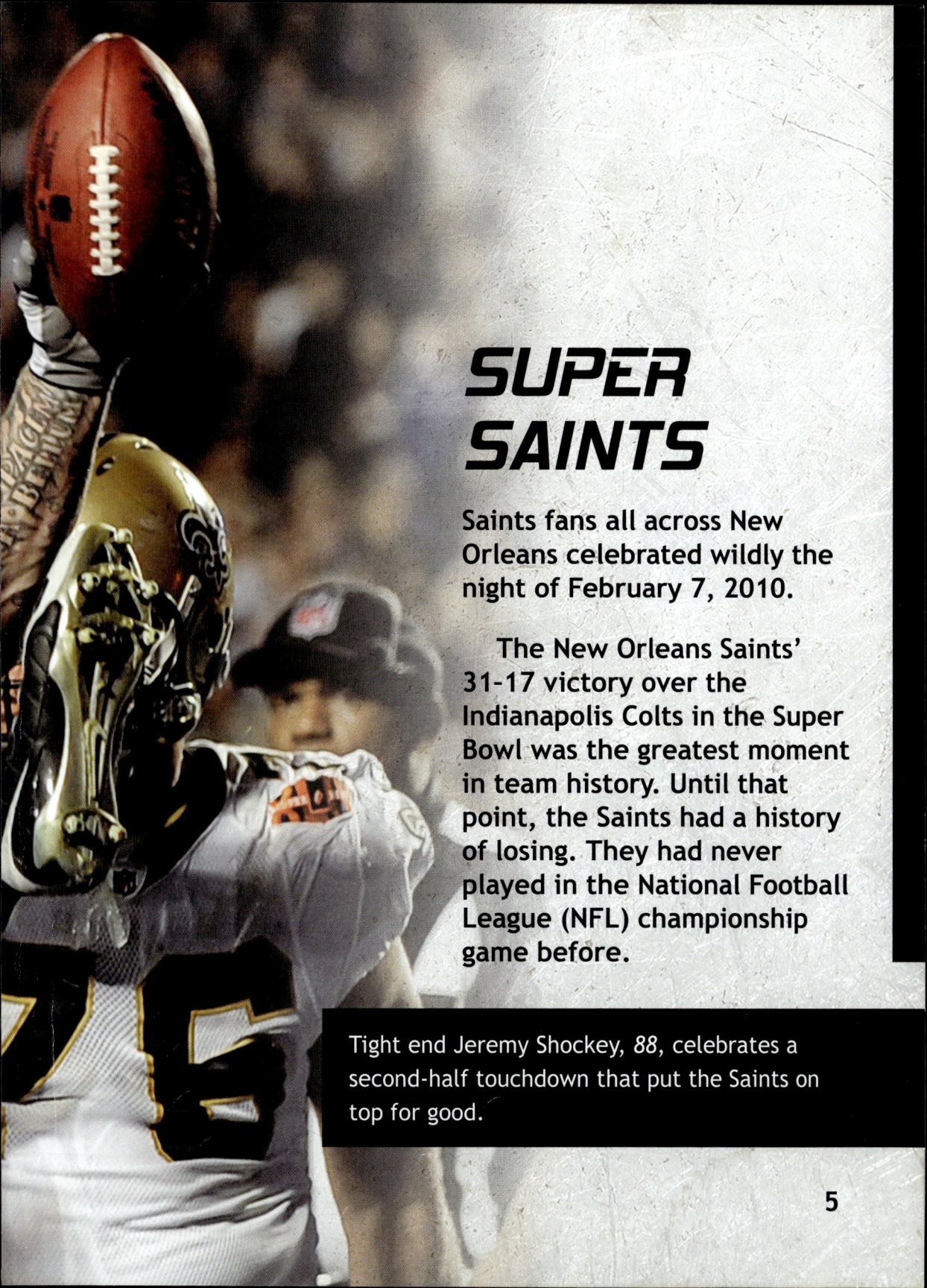

SUPER SAINTS

Saints fans all across New Orleans celebrated wildly the night of February 7, 2010.

The New Orleans Saints' 31-17 victory over the Indianapolis Colts in the Super Bowl was the greatest moment in team history. Until that point, the Saints had a history of losing. They had never played in the National Football League (NFL) championship game before.

Tight end Jeremy Shockey, *88*, celebrates a second-half touchdown that put the Saints on top for good.

5

But this was their night. New Orleans rallied from a 10-0 deficit. They recovered an onside kick to open the third quarter. Things started going their way. The Saints went ahead for good in the fourth quarter. Quarterback Drew Brees found tight end Jeremy Shockey for a 2-yard touchdown pass.

Brees completed 32 of 39 passes for 288 yards and two touchdowns. Cornerback Tracy Porter sealed the game with a late interception return for a touchdown. It was more than just a game to the people of New Orleans, though. It was a symbol of hope.

Tracy Porter returns an interception 74 yards for a touchdown in the Super Bowl.

Drew Brees lifts the Super Bowl trophy.

AT LAST CHAMPIONS!

FAST FACT
Hurricane Katrina caused an estimated $100 billion in damage. Hundreds of thousands of people in Louisiana, Mississippi, and Alabama had to leave their homes.

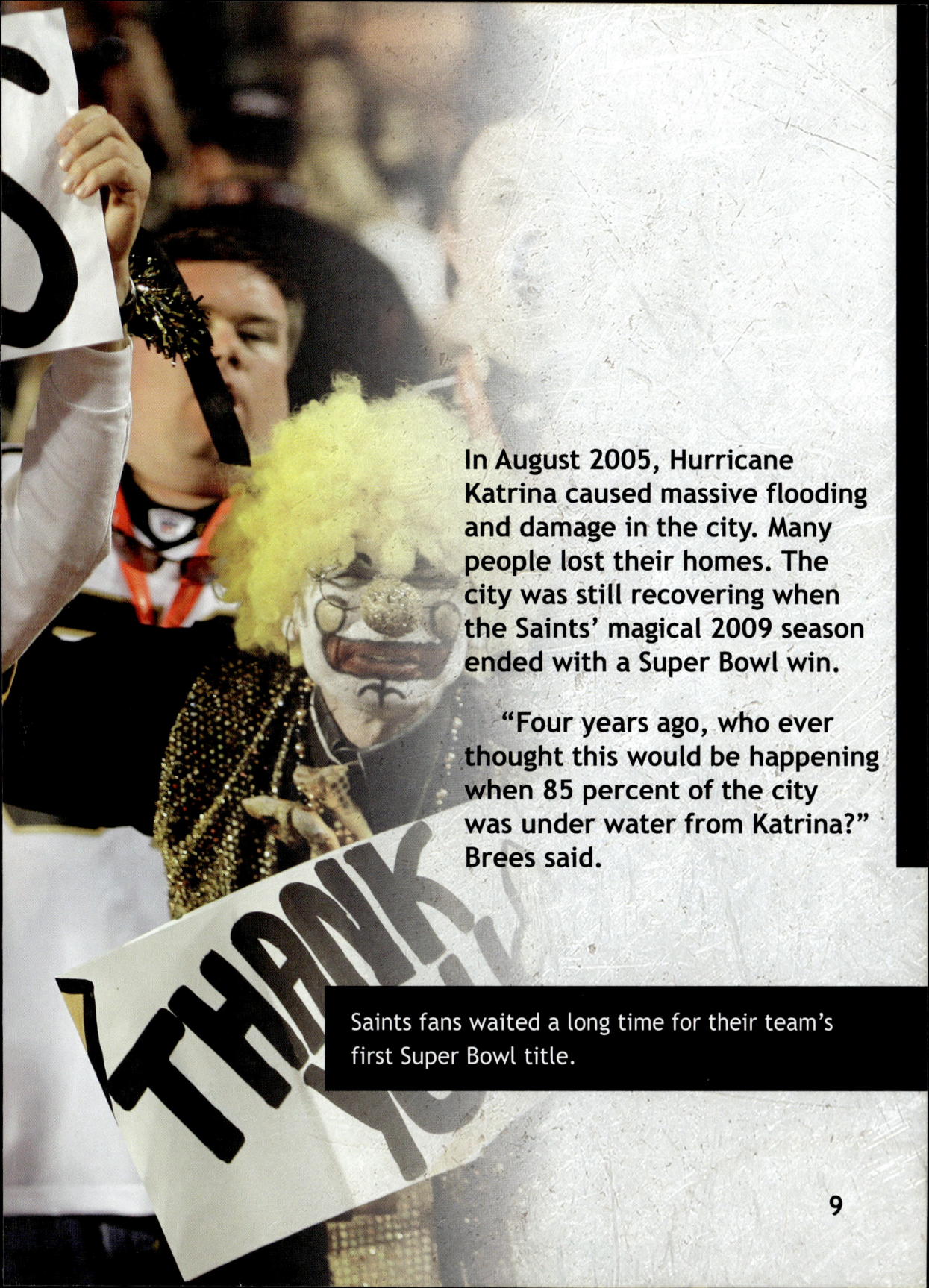

In August 2005, Hurricane Katrina caused massive flooding and damage in the city. Many people lost their homes. The city was still recovering when the Saints' magical 2009 season ended with a Super Bowl win.

"Four years ago, who ever thought this would be happening when 85 percent of the city was under water from Katrina?" Brees said.

Saints fans waited a long time for their team's first Super Bowl title.

FAST FACT The team was announced November 1, 1966. That is All Saints Day in the Catholic Church.

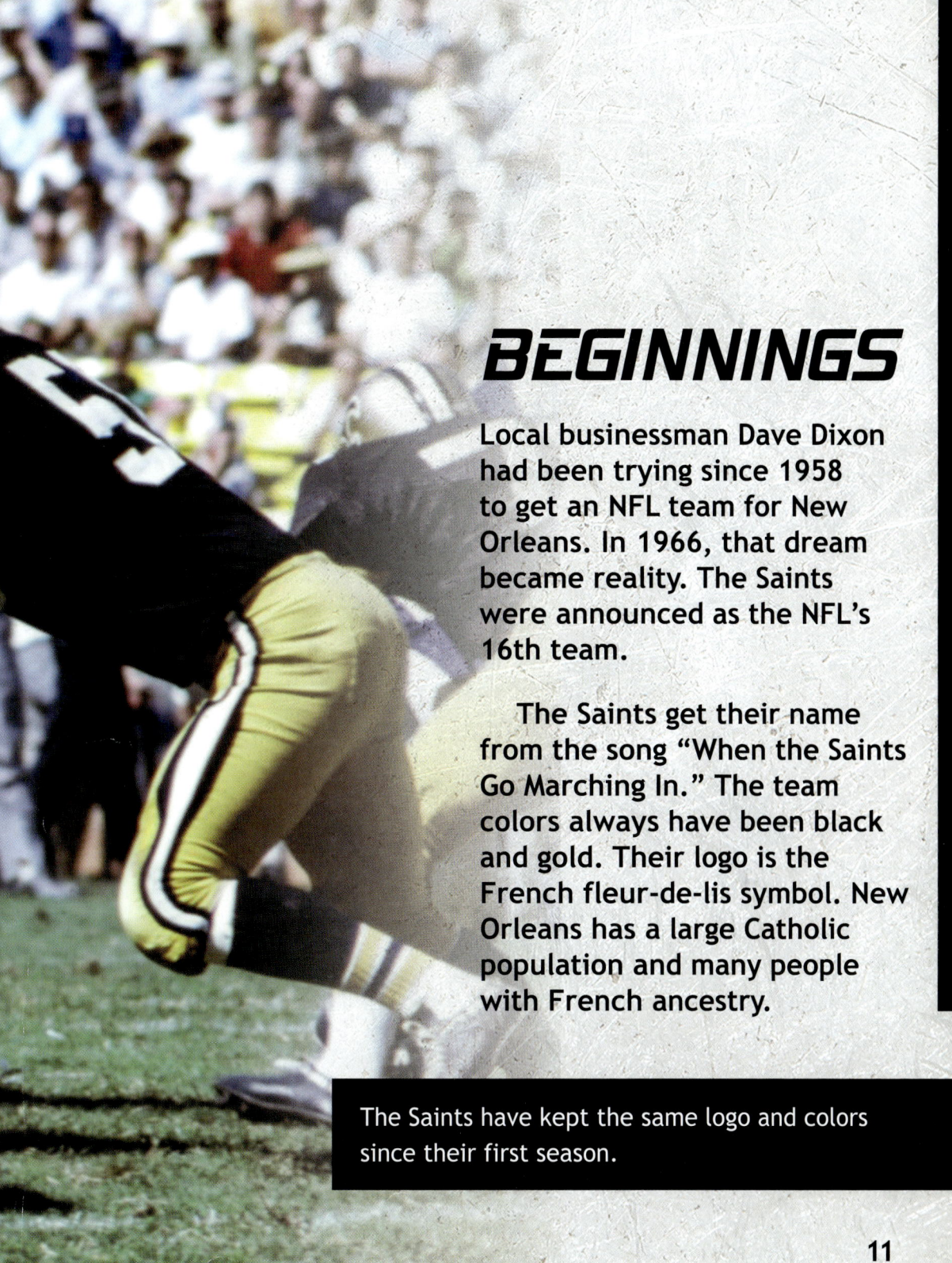

BEGINNINGS

Local businessman Dave Dixon had been trying since 1958 to get an NFL team for New Orleans. In 1966, that dream became reality. The Saints were announced as the NFL's 16th team.

The Saints get their name from the song "When the Saints Go Marching In." The team colors always have been black and gold. Their logo is the French fleur-de-lis symbol. New Orleans has a large Catholic population and many people with French ancestry.

The Saints have kept the same logo and colors since their first season.

The Saints began play in 1967. John W. Mecom Jr. was their first president and owner. Tom Fears was the first coach.

The team played its home games at Tulane Stadium until 1975. That year, the Saints moved into the New Orleans Superdome. They still call the indoor stadium home.

John Gilliam, *42*, returns the opening kickoff 94 yards for a touchdown on the Saints' first-ever play in the NFL.

FAST FACT
In addition to helping found the Saints, Dave Dixon pushed for the Superdome to be built. He later founded the United States Football League. It competed with the NFL in the 1980s.

DOWN YEARS

The people of New Orleans were excited to finally have an NFL team. But for two decades, there wasn't much to cheer for.

The Saints had a losing record in all but two of their first 20 seasons. Their first winning season came in 1987.

The Saints' first home, Tulane Stadium, also hosted three Super Bowls.

FAST FACT
On November 8, 1970, New Orleans kicker Tom Dempsey made an NFL-record 63-yard field goal. That record stood until December 2013.

Kicker Tom Dempsey, *19*, held the NFL record for longest field goal for many years.

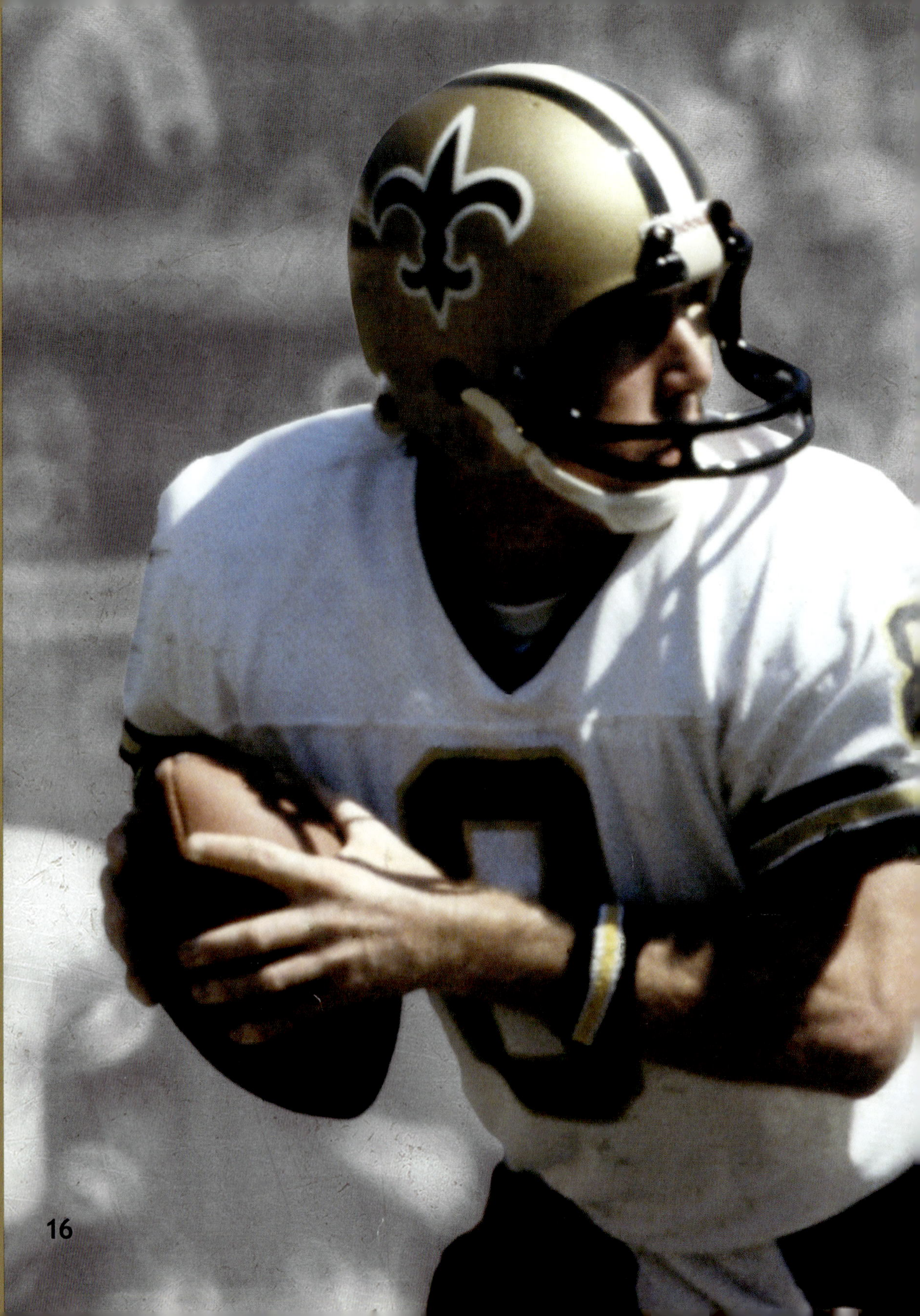

FAST FACT

Archie Manning's sons Peyton Manning and Eli Manning both became Super Bowl-winning quarterbacks.

New professional sports teams have to start from scratch. They often have players who are unwanted by other teams. So new teams often struggle in their early years.

But the Saints did have some great individual performers. Quarterback Archie Manning was one of them. He played for New Orleans from 1971 to 1982. Manning passed for 21,734 yards. That is second only to Drew Brees in team history.

Archie Manning was one of the Saints' best players in his time at quarterback.

MARCHING IN

Tom Benson bought the Saints in 1985. He soon hired Jim Finks as president and general manager. Jim Mora became the coach in 1986. In 1987, New Orleans finally broke through to the playoffs. They went 12-3 before losing to the Minnesota Vikings in their first playoff game.

The Saints made their first playoff appearance after the 1987 season, but they could not get past the Vikings.

19

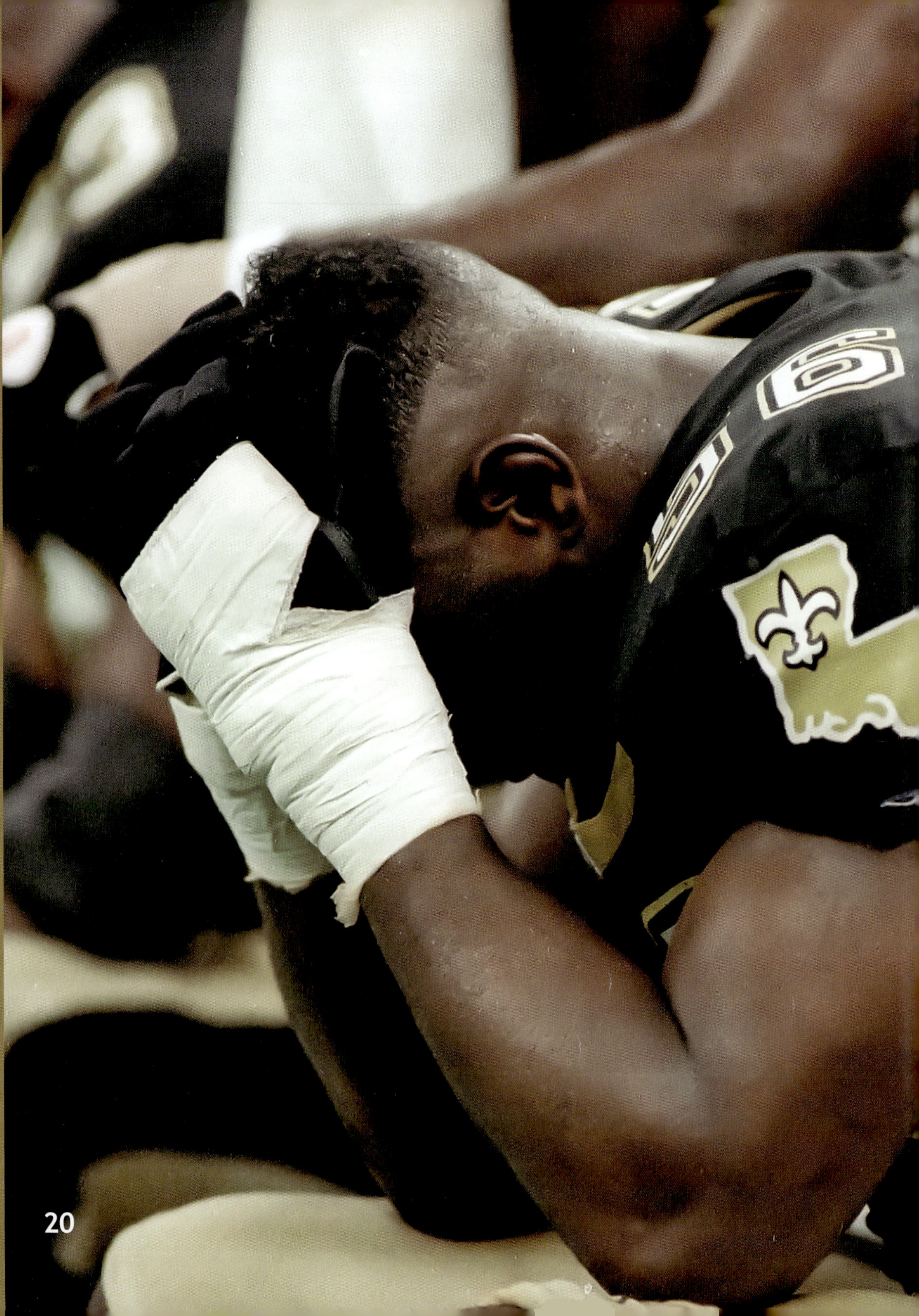

FAST FACT

New Orleans has been to the playoffs 10 times. Their record in those postseason games is 7-9.

The Saints went on a great run starting with the 1987 season. They made the playoffs four out of the next six years. But every time, they lost in the first round.

For a few seasons after, their struggles returned. From 1993 to 1999, New Orleans' best record was 8-8.

The Saints won 12 games in 1992 but went down in the playoffs for the third straight year.

From 1993 to 2005, the Saints made the playoffs just once, losing in the 2000 divisional round. Mora quit in 1996. Mike Ditka and then Jim Haslett followed as Saints coaches. Neither was able to take the team to the top.

Things would soon get better. But first, they got a whole lot worse.

FAST FACT

Running back Deuce McAllister is the Saints' all-time leading rusher. He had 6,096 yards from 2001-2008.

Deuce McAllister had four 1,000-yard rushing seasons for the Saints, including 1,641 in 2003.

STORMS AND SUCCESSES

In 2005, Hurricane Katrina did heavy damage to the Superdome, forcing the Saints out of their home. The team had on-the-field struggles too, finishing the season 3-13.

In 2006, Drew Brees signed with New Orleans. Sean Payton also took over as head coach. It took a few years for the team to build around them and for the team to improve. Finally in 2009, everything came together.

Sean Payton and Drew Brees both came to New Orleans in 2006.

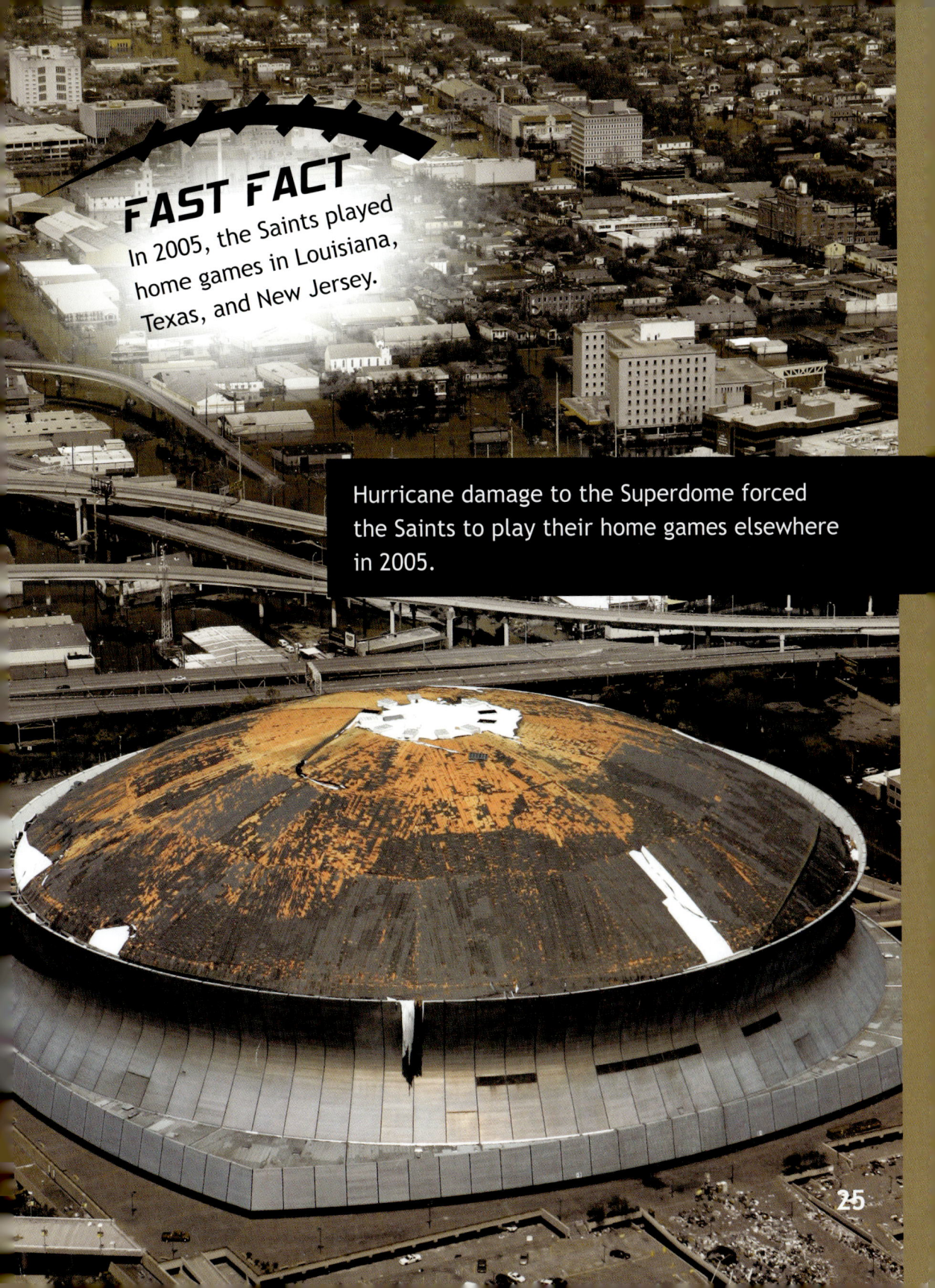

FAST FACT

In 2005, the Saints played home games in Louisiana, Texas, and New Jersey.

Hurricane damage to the Superdome forced the Saints to play their home games elsewhere in 2005.

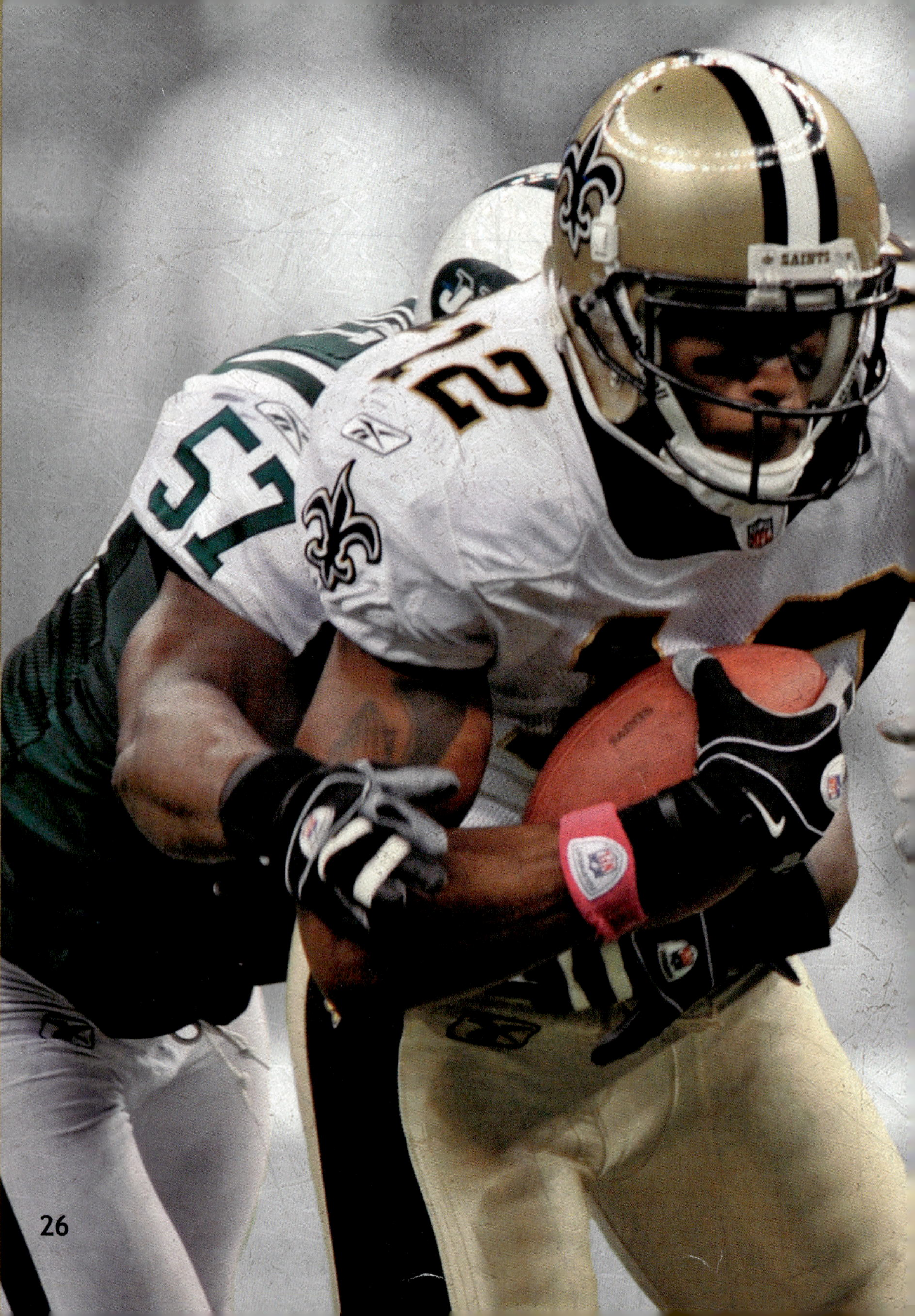

In 2009, Brees had several top receivers in Marques Colston, Devery Henderson, and Jeremy Shockey. Running back Reggie Bush was a star, too. The Saints led the league in scoring. On defense, linebacker Jonathan Vilma and safety Darren Sharper shut opponents down.

New Orleans went 13-3. The Saints finished first in their division. They ended the season with their first NFL championship.

Marques Colston, *12*, was a big part of a 2009 Saints offense that scored the most points in the NFL.

FAST FACT

The Atlanta Falcons are the Saints' biggest rival. Both teams compete in the same division.

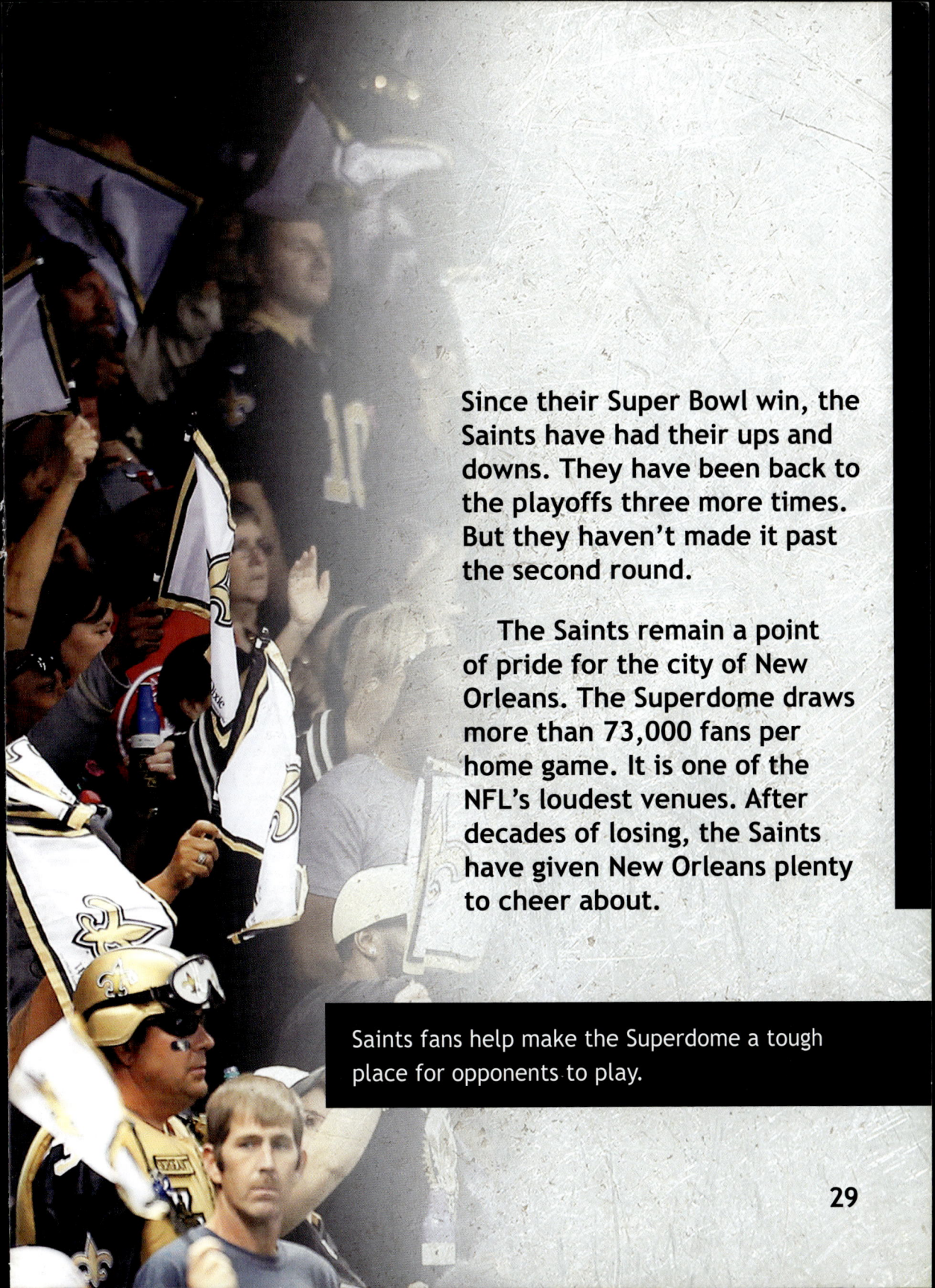

Since their Super Bowl win, the Saints have had their ups and downs. They have been back to the playoffs three more times. But they haven't made it past the second round.

The Saints remain a point of pride for the city of New Orleans. The Superdome draws more than 73,000 fans per home game. It is one of the NFL's loudest venues. After decades of losing, the Saints have given New Orleans plenty to cheer about.

Saints fans help make the Superdome a tough place for opponents to play.

TIMELINE

1966
The NFL awards its 16th team to New Orleans.

1967
The Saints lose their first game 27-13 to the Los Angeles Rams in front of 80,879 people at Tulane Stadium in New Orleans.

1971
New Orleans drafts quarterback Archie Manning second overall in the NFL Draft.

1980
A team-record five players take part in the Pro Bowl.

1988
The Saints' first winning season ends with a playoff loss to the Minnesota Vikings.

2000
New Orleans earns its first playoff win, a 31-28 victory over the St. Louis Rams.

2006
The Saints name Sean Payton their 14th head coach. Quarterback Drew Brees signs with the team.

2006
The Saints beat the rival Atlanta Falcons in their first game back at the Superdome after Hurricane Katrina.

2010
New Orleans beats the Indianapolis Colts 31-17 in the Super Bowl on February 7.

GLOSSARY

CORNERBACK
A defensive player who covers receivers trying to catch passes.

DIVISION
A group of teams that help form a league.

FLEUR-DE-LIS
A flower symbol with three petals that signifies the French royal family.

FREE AGENT
A player who is free to sign with any team.

GENERAL MANAGER
A team employee who makes most decisions regarding the roster.

ONSIDE KICK
A kickoff that is purposely short with the hope that the kicking team can recover the ball.

RIVAL
An opponent with whom a player or team has a fierce and ongoing competition.

SAFETY
A defensive player who covers receivers trying to catch passes.

TIGHT END
An offensive player who sometimes catches passes but is also responsible for blocking.

INDEX

Benson, Tom, 18
Brees, Drew, 4, 6, 7, 9, 17, 24, 27
Bush, Reggie, 27

Colston, Marques, 27

Dempsey, Tom, 14, 15
Ditka, Mike, 22
Dixon, Dave, 11, 13

Fears, Tom, 12
Finks, Jim, 18

Gilliam, John, 12

Haslett, Jim, 22
Henderson, Devery, 27

Manning, Archie, 17
Manning, Eli, 17
Manning, Peyton, 17
McAllister, Deuce, 22, 23
Mecom, Jr., John W., 12
Mora, Jim, 18, 22

New Orleans, Louisiana, 5, 6, 11, 14, 29

Payton, Sean, 24
Porter, Tracy, 6

Sharper, Darren, 27
Shockey, Jeremy, 5, 6, 27
Super Bowl, 5, 7, 9, 14, 17, 29
Superdome, 12, 13, 24, 25, 29

Tulane Stadium, 12, 14

Vilma, Jonathan, 27

ABOUT THE AUTHOR

Phil Ervin was born and raised in Omaha, Nebraska. He has written two other children's sports books and has covered sports for Fox Sports North, the *St. Joseph News-Press*, and the *Forsyth County News*. Ervin attended Benedictine College in Atchison, Kansas.